THE AMISH

THE AMISH

Jean Kinney Williams

American Religious Experience

Franklin Watts
A Division of Grolier Publishing
New York / London / Hong Kong / Sydney
Danbury, Connecticut

Interior design by Molly Heron

Photo Credits ©: Archives of the Mennonite Church: p. 55; Art Resource: p. 20 (Tate Gallery); Black Star: pp. 29, 74 (both photos John Lanois), Blair Seitz: pp. 27, 61, 81, 87; Decent Exposure: pp. 6, 33, 85; Jan Gleysteen Photography: pp. 17, 18, 45, 65, 73; North Wind Picture Archives: p. 14; Pennsylvania Dutch Convention & Visitors Bureau: pp. 8, 31, 38, 43, 53, 77, 82, 97, 101; Photo Researchers: pp. 11 (Eugene Gordon), 25, 35, 41, 48, 89 (all photos Blair Seitz), 58 (Thomas Hollyman), 71 (Jerry Irwin); The Picture Cube Inc.: pp. 42 (Dede Hatch), 51 (Robert W. Ginn), 64 (Robert Echkert Jr.); UPI/Bettmann p. 90.

Library of Congress Cataloging-in-Publication Data

Williams, Jean Kinney.
The Amish / by Jean Kinney Williams.

p.   cm. — (American religious experience)
Summary: Includes a history of the Amish, their general doctrines, practices, social structure, place in American society, changes in beliefs, and issues facing them in modern society.
ISBN 0–531–11275–6
1. Amish—Juvenile literature.   [1. Amish.]   I. Title.   II. Series.
BX8129.A6W55   1996   96–33830
289.7'3—dc20

CIP
AC

CONTENTS

WHO ARE THE AMISH?

Have you ever traveled by car through southeast Pennsylvania, rural parts of the Midwest or Middle Atlantic United States, or Ontario, Canada? You may have noticed the yellow signs that warn drivers to be alert for horse-and-buggy drivers. Who still uses a horse-drawn cart? you might ask yourself.

If you take a turn down one of the side roads, you might see what appears to be an ordinary collection of farms, until you notice one farm that has no automobiles or tractors parked on the property but a big black buggy awaiting its next outing near the horse barn. If it's growing or harvesting season, and it's not a Sunday, you may see one or more men driving horse- or mule-drawn farm equipment through the fields. Look closer at the house and you'll see there are no electric wires running to it from power lines along the roads. Is it sunny and breezy? Then look for a clothesline waving a collection of dark dresses and trousers and boldly colorful shirts, hanging in order of size.

Chances are you've stumbled across an Old Order Amish farm. And if you saw one Amish farm you'll likely spot another, because Amish people, limited by their horse-and-buggy travel, always live in settlements of several (sometimes several hundred) families. The settlements form one or more of their church districts, depending on the number of Amish families in the area.

In the last few decades, tourists have "discovered" the Amish. Each year thousands travel to places like Lancaster County, Pennsylvania, hoping to catch a glimpse of Amish life: the buggies and plows, the severely dressed men and women, smiling children wearing the same kinds of hats and clothing as their parents, or a volleyball match between groups of Amish teens on an afternoon off from chores or paying jobs. (You won't catch Amish teenagers past the age of fourteen or fifteen in school, however. Their "book learning" is considered complete with eighth grade, though they still have much to learn about being Amish.)

The Amish population is 140,000 and always growing. What is it that entices them to reject what we consider necessities? The Amish do without electricity and electronic entertainment like television and radio. They have no central heating or air-conditioning in their homes and, of course, no automobiles. What would your life be like with what seem to be so many limitations? And are the Amish, who use the guarantee of religious freedom in America to reject most of its culture, really content?

More than one hundred years ago, social scientists began predicting that the Amish people, who had emigrated from Europe as farmers in the 1700s and 1800s, and who have always tried to stand apart from the rest of society, would give up their strict ways and make use of the technology that began to emerge in the last century. Living without fine clothing or fancy carriages was one thing, but it was thought that new conveniences like automobiles or electricity would be irresistible. At times, groups of Amish did leave the church to establish different communities that allow for things like tractors or telephones.

But the Old Order Amish population—those who pursue a

more traditional lifestyle—has continued to grow. Its members raise large families that ensure future generations of Old Order Amish church members. What isn't obvious from a quick glance, the kind a tourist might get, is that the Amish don't fight technology or completely reject it. They compromise with it and even adapt some of it for their unique uses.

The Amish don't consider technology bad; their main concern is preserving their close-knit families and communities. One way to do that is by depending on each other and keeping in close, *personal* contact with one another. So while an Amish family has no telephone in their home, and must go to a neighbor's house in order to talk to them, they do use pay telephones or might share a phone with neighbors. They keep it in a "phone shanty," sort of like a private, rural telephone booth, out in a field. (In a more liberal Amish district, there might be a phone inside the barn.) The phone is there for when it's truly needed, but it's not convenient and doesn't disrupt the home.

Because the Amish do not own automobiles, their homes are never far apart from each other. Their closeness allows them to gather for church services every other Sunday at one house or another. (It would take up to an hour to go just a few miles by horse and buggy.) Cars aren't completely rejected; Amish people are allowed to hire a driver to take them to a doctor's office, for example. But they never let it get *too* easy.

Groups of Amish have split off in the past and joined other Anabaptist groups, such as the Mennonite Church. But the complete disappearance of the Old Order Amish never happened as predicted. Today's population, in fact, is three times what it was less than fifty

The Amish have chosen not to use many modern technologies, such as the auto-mobile. But that doesn't mean they are completely separated from society.

years ago. The population remains steady because about 75 to 80 percent of those raised in the faith remain in it as adults.

Who are the Amish, and what keeps their unique way of life so vibrant and growing? How do they maintain their way of life, while surrounded by (even sought out by) modern culture, and what does it have to do with worshipping God? It's easy to look at the Amish in terms of what they don't have. But what have the Amish found to be the advantages of rejecting much of our culture? They are people who, just like everyone else, sometimes have difficult choices to make, and by early adulthood they choose whether or not to stay with the Amish church. Let's go beyond what the tourist might glimpse through a car window. When we see what those choices are really all about, we can then see why the Amish think they have to make them in the first place.

IN EUROPE AND AMERICA

2

An Englishman named William Penn knew what it was like to be persecuted for one's religious beliefs in the late 1600s. In England and Germany, he and other members of the Religious Society of Friends, nicknamed the Quakers, were shown little toleration for their beliefs. This conflict inspired Penn to establish a colony in the "New World" of America. He was determined that Pennsylvania would be a haven to anyone persecuted because of religion, and he traveled along the Rhine River in Europe advertising the new colony. Some of those who heard his invitation were the Anabaptist Mennonites and later their conservative splinter group, the Amish.

Less than two centuries earlier, Christians in western Europe were members of a single church, the Roman Catholic Church. Under its leader, the pope, the Catholic Church had much influence and power in western Europe. But as the Catholic Church itself

William Penn urged many Europeans, including the Anabaptist Mennonites, to settle in the "New World" of America.

went through internal strife, different ideas on religion and calls for church reform became widespread in much of Europe.

In 1517 a Catholic monk and educator in Germany named Martin Luther advocated not only church reform but also new doctrine (or church teachings on God), which was truly revolutionary. The recently invented printing press carried his message throughout Germany. He won support from several German princes, and Protestantism was born.

But one thing hadn't changed. Government and religion still operated as partners, and so while the religion itself was new in some regions, government reaction to those who disagreed with it was still the same—persecution. A group of Christians in Zurich, Switzerland, believed the church reformers hadn't gone far enough, and that government and religion should be completely separate. Though many take this idea for granted today, it was quite radical at the time.

This new group in Zurich thought Christians should model themselves on the Beatitudes that Jesus of Nazareth discussed in his Sermon on the Mount (the Book of Matthew, chapters 5 to 7), which talks of being "peacemakers," "meek," and "clean of heart." They considered infant baptism to be meaningless. Church members, they believed, should be baptized as adults, when their commitment to Christianity was genuine and heartfelt.

This small group of Christians went so far as to rebaptize each other, earning the name Anabaptists, from the Latin term *anabaptismus*, or "baptism again." The Anabaptists also refused to serve in the military, wanting to lead nonviolent lives as they believed Jesus tells all Christians to do. In an era when the government called for strict obedience to the church it was aligned with, and with war rampant between the various governments in Europe, many people could not tolerate the nonviolence of the Anabaptists.

When prison sentences, fines, and exile didn't stop the growing Anabaptist movement in Switzerland and southern Germany, torture and execution were tried. Some Anabaptists were even sold to serve as galley slaves on the Mediterranean Sea. Hundreds of Anabaptists were killed in the sixteenth century, but this ferocious reaction of the Swiss city governments only made the Anabaptists more resolved to remain apart from the violent world. In the meantime, Anabaptist beliefs spread into northern Germany and the Netherlands.

In 1536 a Dutch Catholic priest, Menno Simons, was converted to the Anabaptist movement and became an influential leader. He reaffirmed their nonviolent and antimilitary stance. He also advocated "shunning," or having no contact with those who had left the Anabaptist Church or were openly violating its rules. Within a few decades, the Anabaptists in northern Europe became known as Mennonites.

During the first quarter of the seventeenth century, the persecution of the Anabaptists decreased as arguments among themselves increased. The divisive issue was shunning: some thought it too harsh, while others considered it necessary to keep the church intact. Still looking for a land where they might practice their religion in relative peace, many Anabaptists began moving down the Rhine River to new lands. They settled in two main regions: a war-devastated area known as the Palatinate, now part of Germany, and Alsace, today a province of France. They were renowned for their skill at farming. Soon they enjoyed more tolerance as they helped replenish food supplies to parts of Europe torn apart in the mid-1600s by the Thirty Years' War.

Menno Simons became a leader of the Anabaptists in Europe.

By the late 1600s the Anabaptists still held to their goal of remaining separate from the world, but a young Swiss church elder, Jakob Ammann, thought church discipline was too lax. He convinced them to hold a communion service twice instead of once a year and to include in it a foot-washing ceremony, reminding church members of Jesus' Last Supper. But his insistence that church discipline include the practice of strict shunning caused a division that never healed, despite Ammann's attempts a few years later to rejoin the Mennonite Church.

Though Ammann's actions and leadership formed a new church, whose members came to be called the Amish, little is known about him. His influence, however, is felt today. Church members still hold to shunning baptized members who leave the church, for example. They also wear simple (what the Amish refer to as "plain") fashions and even the hook-and-eye fasteners on clothing that Ammann recommended over fancy buttons. But what became of him after 1712, when all Anabaptists were ordered to leave Markirch in Alsace, is not known.

By that time emigration to the New World was catching on all over Europe. The Amish were no more immune to this fever than anyone else. The Amish were among the German people who began leaving Germany and the Palatinate in the early 1700s. War, high

---

At first, Anabaptists did not think of themselves as farmers. After moving into Rhineland regions such as the Palatinate, however, they developed farming techniques so well that they became known as the best farmers in Europe.

taxes, and economic hardship in that area made many feel as though they had no choice but to emigrate. The government in Bern, Switzerland, angry with their refusal to serve in the military, even tried exporting Anabaptists to Holland. From there many Mennonites and Amish emigrated to America.

The ship *Charming Nancy* arrived in America in 1737 with twenty-one Amish families aboard. Altogether, about a hundred Amish families came to America in the next thirty years and settled in Pennsylvania. Today, Lancaster County is the second largest Amish settlement in North America. A larger number came between 1815 and 1860, many of them ending up in the Midwest. None of the Amish who chose to stay in Europe retained their traditional way of life. Instead they joined Mennonite congregations or assimilated into the mainstream culture. Even Jakob Ammann's daughter rejoined a state church.

In America the Amish had to struggle with all the difficulties of the new land, from carving out farmland to conflicts with American Indian groups. They also were under pressure to fight in the Revolutionary War. Other religious groups lured many Amish away, and the church itself has splintered into different factions.

Jakob Ammann encouraged Anabaptists to include a foot-washing ceremony in the communion service. Jesus had washed the disciples' feet at the Last Supper to suggest that they go out and spread his teachings. As he states it in the Book of John, chapter 13: "If I then, your Lord and Teacher, have washed your feet, you also ought to wash one another's feet. For I have given you an example, that you also should do as I have done to you."

Despite the hardships of America, the Amish were allowed to own land for the first time. They also had the freedom to move from one place to another, which they did when one community faced too much pressure or temptation from the world around them. They had found a country where they could use their farming skills, practice their religion, and continue their unique way of life.

Today, the Amish are found in more than twenty states and one province of Canada, as far west as Montana, north as far as Minnesota, Ontario, and upstate New York, and as far south as Florida and Texas. The three largest settlements, or groups of church districts, are in Ohio and Pennsylvania, each with more than two hundred districts, and Indiana, with more than one hundred districts. There often are "plain" groups with Anabaptist origins, such as the Mennonites, with similar church rules as the Old Order Amish living nearby. A variety of other Amish and Mennonite church communities make more use of technology.

The Old Order Amish church has survived these splinters and is now more than three hundred years old. Though it's been 250 years since they left Europe, the Amish people have managed to hold on to their cultural roots. They still speak a German dialect called Pennsylvania German or Dutch (the word for German is *Deutsch)* in the home; children don't learn English until they go to first grade, usually in their own Amish school. The hymns they sing at their church services were written by Anabaptists imprisoned 450 years ago.

THE AMISH
WAY OF LIFE

3

et's go back to that quiet country road and the Amish family's farm with no tractor or cars, electric wires, or TV satellite dish in the yard. One of the first things you may notice is a stunning flower garden near the house. Then you might notice something else: the quiet. No air-conditioning hum, no radio or television coming from the house or work areas, no telephones ringing.

Who lives here? Chances are it's a large family: Amish families *average* seven children. Almost one-fourth have ten or more children, and there may even be grandparents living in a smaller, separate *daadi* (grandparent) house on the farm. Loneliness is not something Amish children are familiar with.

In front of many homes in Amish communities are beautiful lawns and gardens.

In addition to many siblings, there are probably many cousins, aunts, and uncles in the neighborhood. A child's mother and father are likely within hollering distance, too, since the Amish consider it important to have both parents work at home as role models for their children. Amish children know they are different from most other American children, but surrounded by so many Amish relatives and neighbors they are quite at home in their small communities.

As the world around that community changes, Amish children always know what is expected of them. They know what kind of clothing they can wear, so there's no argument about that in the morning. They know what chores they have to do each day, and they know their help is an important contribution to the family's livelihood. They know weddings will come when farmwork is finished in the fall. They don't have to wonder if their parents' marriage will ever end in divorce, because divorce is not considered a solution to marital troubles.

The life of an Amish person, family, or community is governed by an unwritten but well-understood set of rules called the *Ordnung*. This German word, roughly translated, means "an order of the whole way of life," according to sociologist Donald Kraybill, who has spent several years studying the Lancaster County Amish.[1] The Ordnung can vary from one Amish church district to another, and it has slowly evolved over the years.

Some commonly followed Ordnung "musts" include: the type of clothing men and women, girls and boys can wear; the color and style of buggies; the use of the German dialect in the home and workplace and proper German during church services; steel wheels on buggies or farm equipment; and marriage only to another Amish church member.

From a very early age, boys and girls know what to expect in day-to-day life, such as what to wear.

Some Ordnung "must nots" are: tractors in the fields; owning a car; using electricity from power lines; central heat, telephones, or wall-to-wall carpet in the home; high school education; air travel; jewelry; and divorce.

The Ordnung can change as needed. When telephones became available in American homes, for example, the Amish tried them as eagerly as anyone, but church leaders gradually decided against the new technological gadget. Two generations ago, an Amish father who took a job in a factory faced excommunication from the church, but today—as farmland slips away to increasing development and sky-rockets in price—a factory job is not uncommon among Amish men. And children now might wear black sneakers, once forbidden.

Another German word that helps define Amish life is *Gelassenheit*. It embodies qualities such as humility, simplicity, and submission. An Amish child learns to submit to his or her parents' authority; an Amish wife acknowledges her husband's role as head of the family; an Amish husband knows that church ministers and the bishop are authorities over him; and all of them consider their way of life to be a submission to Amish tradition and an offering to God.

Gelassenheit is not a word the Amish use much, if at all, but it's a quality they recognize by how a person presents her or himself. Someone with a loud, boisterous laugh who likes to draw attention certainly is not practicing the quality of Gelassenheit. On the other hand, the Amish don't go in much for obvious politeness, either, considering it an attempt to be fancy. So, although in general they are a friendly people, you seldom hear a "please" or "thank you" in conversation.

The Amish household is generally much quieter than a non-Amish home, because there are no electronic appliances and also

The Amish household is usually pretty quiet, even at dinner. This quiet is one example of Gelassenheit—*a belief in humility and simplicity.*

because conversation is quieter. Sundays with no church service are spent at home relaxing, doing only necessary work, or visiting friends or relatives. Each day the dinner hour is often a quiet one. It begins with each family member saying a silent prayer of thanks, after which there is little talk just for the sake of conversation (though sometimes belching isn't unusual—it's a sign of a good appetite and isn't considered impolite). Time spent around the dinner table is more likely to be used by various family members to discuss farm or other family business operations.

Gelassenheit isn't just a matter of being calm and quiet. It's a whole approach to life in which the individual is not the most important person in the world, even to himself or herself. Donald Kraybill found "a widely used school motto" to be **JOY**: **J**esus is first, **Y**ou are last, and **O**thers are in between.[2] No doubt all children in large families, not just among the Amish, soon learn that a "me first" attitude must give way to patience and waiting. But it's also likely that those non-Amish children will live next door to or go to school with children who live the "me first" life. The Amish, though, practice the **JOY** approach to living throughout the community. So even children from an unusually small Amish family will grow up much the same as their large-family peers: sharing bedrooms, having only a few toys, and learning to cooperate with others.

Growing up in a large family, usually with a family-run business as well, Amish children learn how to work at an early age. But they spend their first two years basking in loads of love and attention, with no scoldings or spankings. Many Amish babies are born at home with a midwife attending. There are no baby showers or christenings, but all babies are welcome in the world. A baby means a new family member to help at home someday and, parents hope, a future church member.

By age two, a child begins to experience the discipline and authority that will carry her or him to Amish adulthood. Young children learn to obey their parents and are given small tasks to do around the home or farm, perhaps learning from an older sibling.

Children often do their chores alongside their parents or each other. They learn cooperation in everything they do.

While the mother of a family is the primary caretaker of the young children, the father's presence at home is also considered important for Amish children to learn what will be expected of them someday. And a young child also learns patience by sitting through three-hour church services.

School-aged children, whom the Amish call "scholars," are beginning to learn more of the roles they will play as adults. By age six, girls are helping their mothers with younger children, gardening, or housework, and boys are spending more time on farmwork with their fathers, milking cows, or carrying wood. Everyone gets up by five or six o'clock to do chores before school. Children learn to work as they enjoy family camaraderie. In the book *A Day in the Life of the Amish*, an Amish mother of twelve writes that when she did the laundry, a job she usually assigns to her daughters, the girls teased her: "Mother is going to do the laundry. She probably doesn't even know how! How many years was it since she last washed? It was probably 50 years ago!"[3] An Amish child learns about cooperation, rather than competition, at home, school, and church.

Not all time outside of school is spent working. There are no swim clubs or sports leagues, but children can swim in ponds or play softball or volleyball. Time for these games comes at recess or on holidays, such as the Monday after Easter (but generally not on Sundays). In the winter, sledding and skating are popular. Children spend time with friends or cousins on Sundays and get to break up their routines with weddings and auctions. Though they shun "the

---

Although children have a lot of responsibilities at home, they usually find time for games such as volleyball.

world," the Amish appreciate nature, the seasons, and animals as God's creations, and some Amish families take trips to the zoo.

When school ends for Amish youths, after eighth grade, they probably will begin looking for work. They may be hired by their parents or by another Amish business or perhaps by a restaurant, factory, or plant nursery. They might contribute to the family's income with their own wages or save money for their future. This is an age when Amish youths are too old for school but not ready to be baptized and commit themselves to the Old Order Amish way of life. It can be an anxious time for Amish parents, just as it is for parents of any teenagers.

During this part of their lives, Amish youths are very involved with their peers and usually join up with a "crowd," or "courting" group of young Amish men and women. It could have as many as two hundred members. Each group gives itself a name, such as (in Lancaster County) the Canaries or the Kirkwoods, named for a nearby small town. The group reflects the range from liberal to conservative Amish families and church districts. Also, it is from this group that members will likely meet a future spouse. One way they get together is by holding "singings" on Sunday evenings at the same home where church services had been held.

After fifteen years in a very structured environment, Amish youths at this age are given considerable freedom by their parents. Ahead of these young people is a major decision: Will they join the Amish church in a few years? Those who leave the church and the community before they are baptized are not shunned, because they have broken no vows to maintain Amish tradition and rules.

Young Amish people have spent their whole lives learning to follow their families' rules, but parents know the choice to become Amish belongs to each person. So adults often look the other way

These young men are on their way to a Sunday evening "singing."

temporarily as their young people get a taste of the outside world. Amish teenagers might go to a nearby town and see a movie, organize a dance, buy non-Amish clothes to wear away from home, or, among boys especially, drive or even secretly own a car. In the larger settlements, the crowds can get downright rowdy, hold dances with drinking, and embarrass their families. But as the sociologist John Hostetler observed, this is the only period in their life when Amish people are permitted to rebel. They spend these teenage years bonding with the people with whom they will spend the rest of their lives.

"It usually seems if you have a well-rounded family, and the children step out of the Amish life for awhile," they return to the fold very pro-Amish, said one Amish father of nine. Among his baptized children, his oldest son had a hard time accepting the conservative lifestyle. It is a very difficult decision for some to make. A strong desire to pursue an education, for example, might eventually lead some Amish youths away from their traditional roots. About 20 to 25 percent of those raised Amish will not join the church as young adults, often joining a Mennonite church instead.

Some young people leave the church if their own parents leave it. In other cases, one young person's decision not to join may influence other family members to leave, too. John Hostetler, who himself left the Amish church prior to baptism, interviewed a former Amish woman who had felt so out of place with her young Amish peers that she was physically ill until she left the community to continue her education. Having tasted the world, though, most young Amish come to appreciate their Old Order upbringing and the close sense of community that can be difficult to find in modern America. A young married Amish man told Donald Kraybill: "The close family ties are the thing that really draw you back."[4]

Each September, Old Order Amish church districts baptize young men and women in their late teens or around twenty years old. It is a solemn ceremony, in which they promise to embrace Jesus and reject the world outside their Amish faith. They may now marry but only within their faith. Since a high percentage of Amish marry, and then have large families, each young person's baptismal vows are like a promise to help the Amish faith continue to grow and prosper. Their standing in the Amish community will increase with marriage and children. As they age, they gain authority and esteem, remaining a vital part of their church district.

Each Amish home is a small version of their larger community: a place where people committed to the Ordnung and living a different life than most of the people around them can feel secure in knowing they belong and are valued.

DIFFICULT CHOICES

Our view of the Amish is sometimes ironic. Looking into their world, we can envy them for the social and family security they have, but we also feel relieved when we can go on about our lives in a world full of choices. Individualism, after all, is as American a tradition as fireworks on the Fourth of July. What we may not realize is that the Amish, by accepting their lack of choices, can enjoy a strong sense of security.

For example, many American women or teenage girls would bristle at the suggestion that their goal should be to marry, have children, and work hard primarily as a wife and mother. But that is what Amish girls learn from childhood, and it is what most of them decide to do with their lives when they become baptized members of the Amish church. But is it really that cut-and-dried?

Yes, Amish women are expected to obey their husbands. But because this is a people whose daily lives are examples of their religious beliefs (**JOY**, remember), husbands are expected to treat wives with respect and consideration. In an important family matter, husband and wife generally will make joint decisions. Domestic violence is very rare among the Amish. When some kind of abusive situation becomes public knowledge, offenders are reprimanded or possibly excommunicated.

Amish women are committed to, not offended by, their role as homemaker in their families and communities. Families are encouraged by church leaders to avoid restaurants and eat at home, so women are apt to spend much time fixing meals for their large families. We might grab a can of soup or frozen dinner from the grocery store for a quick lunch, but an Amish woman will probably pull something she canned herself off her pantry shelf. Although electricity from power lines is banned in Amish homes, an Amish kitchen can look surprisingly modern. Women may use gas-powered stoves and refrigerators, sewing machines, and washing machines. Disposable diapers and cake mixes aren't unheard of in Amish homes, either.

Amish women are in charge of the house and yard work: sewing and washing the family's clothing, gardening, and mowing the grass using push mowers. One woman voiced this mild complaint to Kraybill: "If the men would mow the lawns, there would be engines on them, and I am sure there would be."[1]

While ideas like "careers" and "feminism" have negative value in Amish society, women find many ways to express individuality and make significant contributions to the family's income. Wives in charge of the vegetable garden often set aside produce to sell in addition to what they preserve for the family to consume. When Sam Stoltzfus's telephone answering machine picks up a call to the phone shanty he shares with his oldest son's family, callers hear infor-

The pantry or cellar is a winter storehouse for preserved fruits and vegetables.

mation about his wife's horseradish business as well as his gazebo business.

Psychologist and artist Sue Bender spent several weeks with two Amish families in Iowa and Ohio in the 1980s, an experience she wrote about in her book *Plain and Simple*. In Ohio she stayed with a family whose wife and mother, Becky, found a way to remain

Amish and still pursue a strong interest in medicine. Becky read an article in the Amish weekly newspaper, the *Budget,* about an Amish woman in Iowa who ran a birthing center. Becky's husband agreed to let her spend time there to learn more about this type of work. She then began her own birthing center for the Amish women in her community, under the supervision of a doctor.

Women also express creativity with their famous Amish quilts, which make use of vibrant colors contrasted with black or other

Each of these quilts requires about a hundred hours of work, but for these women it is a labor of love and a way to express their creativity. The quilts are often donated to charity auctions.

dark colors. Some of these quilts sell for hundreds of dollars. But Ms. Bender found that, like many others, Amish women enjoyed in general the role they played in their family and community. Of one wife, Ms. Bender observed, "All her duties were an expression of her love for her family and for God. The extra hours she spent quilting tiny stitches expressed her love for the person who would receive the quilt."[2]

Sacrifice for one another is a hallmark of many families and religious communities, but for the Amish interdependence is intentionally built into their way of life. Members of an Amish church district live close to one another, and their families may have been in the area for more than a generation. Though the Amish pay local real estate and federal income taxes, they reject government assistance such as welfare or social security, even for their elderly. Among the Amish, the elderly and physically or mentally handicapped are cared for by extended family members. A church district's alms fund is reserved for families in financial need.

One incident among the Iowa Amish gave Sue Bender a different viewpoint on dependence: "I remembered one late June afternoon when Eli returned from the blacksmith shop and told me that rain had been predicted for the next day. We went from farm to farm helping his neighbors collect hay from the field and then move it into their barns. After a hearty meal at the last farmhouse we

---

A barn raising is an incredible example of the teamwork and interdependence of people in an Amish community. A hundred men working together can erect a barn in one day.

returned home tired but happy. The crop was saved."[3] Because several types of modern farm equipment are off-limits to Amish men, they must often rely on one another.

The Amish compare participation in commercial insurance programs to electric company hookup: dependence on an organization outside the community. But they can participate in their own insurance programs, which members voluntarily run. If a bolt of lightning causes a barn to burn to the ground, Amish insurance will pay for new building materials. But much of the labor to build a new barn is volunteered by men of the community, and wives will spend the day cooking and serving the laborers. Help, in fact, can arrive by buggy from miles away, as people take advantage of the opportunity to spend a day together. They enjoy visiting as they work and know they will receive the same help if they ever need it.

Like their children, Amish adults don't spend all their time working. They take time for their friendships. They correspond with friends and family out of easy visiting reach, so mail delivery is an anticipated time each day. Many enjoy reading and contributing to the Old Order newspapers, the *Budget* and *Die Botschaft* ("The Message"), which are full of news about other church districts. Amish magazines such as *Family Life* have features for adults and children and poetry by Amish contributors. And adults enjoy breaks in their routines as much as children, with weddings, auctions, or quiltings.

Acceptance of which technology is or isn't off-limits has brought about splits among the Amish. The label "Old Order" was added in the nineteenth century as their clothing and lifestyle became more distinguishable from those of other Americans. Early in that century, Amish bishops and ministers dealt with members who wanted to wear fancy or expensive clothing, decorate their homes with lavish furniture, or perhaps meet in meetinghouses instead of each others' homes. But with the advent of electricity, telephones, and automobiles, what should be allowed became a more challenging issue for church leaders.

One schism occurred in 1910 in Lancaster County, when a group of about thirty-five Amish families wanted a more lenient interpretation of shunning but were denied. This group became known as "Peachey" Amish (named after two of their ministers). They began using electricity, telephones, and tractors. In a few more years, they were driving cars and worshipping in church buildings. In 1950 they joined another group that had split from the Old Order body, the Beachy Amish. Today there are several Beachy Amish congregations in Lancaster County. They may use meeting-houses for church services in English and drive cars, but they still wear plain clothing and men wear short beards.

A more recent split among the Old Order Amish occurred in 1966 in Lancaster. About one hundred families broke away, partly over disagreements about farm equipment, and other districts in the Midwest followed suit. Today there are several affiliations living among Old Order Amish. Called the "New Order Amish," this group approaches family life conservatively by forbidding tobacco use and keeping a close eye on courting activities among their youths. The families still get around by horse and buggy, meet for church in their homes, and worship in German, but some make use of tractors, in-home telephones, and electricity.

How do they decide which technology is OK and which isn't? Bishops try to consider the long-term effects that acceptance of a new technology or lifestyle will have. When cars became available

The Amish have to decide whether or not to use different types of technology. One reason for not using it is that they can simply live without it. This boy can mow the lawn beautifully with a horse-drawn mower, for example.

early in the twentieth century, they were something only the wealthy could afford. To the Amish the car was a symbol of wealth and pride. Later, it was feared that automobiles would tempt the Amish away from their communities. Riding in one is allowed (though often not on Sunday, depending on the district), but driving one and especially owning one can mean automatic expulsion from the church.

Central heating is forbidden because, theoretically, a family might spend less time together. With one kerosene heater or wood-stove keeping one or two rooms warm at a time, families congregate in the same couple of rooms. Wall-to-wall carpeting is considered extravagant, though area rugs in a room are allowed. Hookup to public utilities creates a dependence on those companies, and it's a link between the Amish family and the "world" from which they are to live apart. Not allowing tractors in the fields means an Amish farm is only as big as can be worked by horse or mule. An Amish farmer told Kraybill one reason the Old Order bishops continue to ban tractors was "if we allow big equipment we'll go into more debt and need more land to pay it off."[4] Not having machines also ensures that more men, who would otherwise be replaced by the machines, stay employed.

Some rules are unchanged because they maintain the Amish identity. Going without stylish clothing, for example, is an offering the Amish make to God, and an example of Gelassenheit: submitting to the established order, rather than a personal preference. All men are required to wear hats outside the house, for example. An Amish person's clothing can also express how conservative or liberal their church district is. How wide is the man's hat brim? More conservative groups will require a wider brim, and one group, in west-central Pennsylvania, allows men to wear only one suspender. How long is a woman's dress, or how close fitting is it? A woman from a more liberal district might have the correct plain-colored dress, but it might be a shade lighter, made from a fancier material, or be shorter and fit her figure more closely than that of a woman whose district is more conservative.

In general, Amish men cut their hair even with their earlobes and wear bangs over their foreheads. They are clean-shaven until marriage or, if still single, until age forty. Their beards grow untrimmed, but no mustaches are allowed: in the church's early days in Europe, mustaches were associated with the military. Men wear straw hats in summer and black felt hats other times. Belts on trousers aren't allowed. Suits are black, with hook-and-eye fasteners. Dress shirts can be white or vivid colors such as burgundy, green, blue, or purple.

Amish women keep their heads covered at almost all times, symbolizing their submission to God and men. A simple white cap is worn most of the time, and a black cap or bonnet is worn to church. Their hair remains uncut, parted in the middle and worn in a bun. Women use snaps or straight pins to fasten their dresses, which are the same dark colors as men's shirts. They wear an apron over the dress. A woman or girl never wears pants. A triangle-shaped cape is always worn to church. The aprons were designed for pregnant women and the capes for nursing mothers, but all women wear both.

Makeup is forbidden, as is jewelry, even wedding bands. Every detail of one's appearance signifies one's humility or pride. In only two cases have the Amish accepted twentieth-century changes in

The Amish dress in similar, simple clothing so that clothes will not be a source of pride. This is another expression of Gelassenheit.

dress: children wear sneakers, and some clothing is made from synthetic fabrics (this cuts back on ironing for an Amish woman or her daughters). Other than the sneakers, young children are dressed much the same as their parents.

Another important symbol of the Amish culture is the horse. Making the horse their main source of transportation and farm power is another offering to God: it limits the Amish family's horizons and keeps their farms small. It shows the world that the Amish are determined to maintain their slower pace, no matter how fast the world changes around them. Sue Bender wrote about an hour-long buggy ride she took after being accustomed to getting around in a car. She savored the scenery that drifted by and the rhythm of the horse's clip-clop on the road. Symbolic of that slower pace, her Amish host's buggy dashboard had no clock on it, but a calendar.

All Amish drive more or less the same type of buggy, so even wealthy Amish families will have the same kind of transportation as those with less money. As more Amish are required to look beyond farming to support their families, the horse remains as a shared link to their past. The horse links people to each other, even as work among the Amish becomes more varied.

And the horse isn't just a symbol. It can practically become a member of the family. In the book *A Day in the Life of the Amish,* a woman in Kentucky writes of their horses: "We have two sorrel Belgian workhorses, 'May' and 'Minnie.' Our faithful driving horse, 'Diane' (we call her Di for short), is 16 years old. I dread to think when we can't use her anymore."[5] Former Amish schoolteacher Sara Fisher would hear boys at recess "brag about their horses and compare their different traits."[6]

While the Amish do what they can to remain apart from the

The horse is a mode of transportation, a hard worker, a link to the past, and a symbol of the slow pace in the Amish culture.

world, they usually have at least some "English," or non-Amish, neighbors or other acquaintances with whom they are friendly. They are quick to help non-Amish friends in time of need, just as they would help other Amish. But because the Amish don't join organizations such as scouts, 4-H clubs, organized sports leagues, or most professional organizations, the contacts are limited.

Conflict with military service was one reason so many Amish left Europe in the 1700s and 1800s. It has often proved to be a problem for them in the United States, too. Amish men who serve as soldiers in the military will be excommunicated from the church. In general, Amish men declare themselves conscientious objectors (COs) in time of war. During World War I, their commitment to this policy was given a harsh test. The United States entered the international war in the spring of 1917, and a military draft to build up the armed services began shortly after. While the government had a vague provision for conscientious objectors, all men drafted had to report to training camps, where it was hoped that, away from home, COs would submit to pressure and put on a soldier's uniform.

The Amish men who resisted that pressure were subject to beatings and a variety of penalties for not donning a uniform. At home, Amish were harassed because of their antimilitary beliefs and their use of a German dialect. Germany was the main aggressor of the war, and there were intense anti-German feelings all over the United States, so it was assumed the Amish were German sympathizers.

A better alternative was worked out by World War II, when 94 percent of the Amish men drafted declared themselves COs. In the United States and Canada they were put to work in hospitals, for example, or given farm deferments. Another conscientious objec-

Some Amish men who were conscientious objectors in World War II were sent to work in hospitals far from home, in this case serving in a mental hospital.

tor program that began after World War II, called the "1-W" pro-gram, put COs to work in city hospitals far from home and Amish roots. Many did not return to their communities. By 1969 a group of Amish representatives worked out an agreement with the feder-al government allowing Amish men to work on Amish-run farms at least 50 miles (80 km) from their homes rather than join the army.

Other conflicts with laws and regulations have erupted in recent years. The Amish have worked with the federal government to become exempt from paying into the Social Security system or receiving payments from it. They even lobbied the Department of Labor to allow their men working on construction sites not to wear hard hats. The hats are a safety precaution but a violation of the Ordnung. As the world around them continues to change, the Amish continue to adapt to and seek compromises with it.

KEEPING
THE FAITH

5

he Amish value hard work, and the one aspect of their lives at which they work hardest is their Christian faith. An Amish adult doesn't spend hours each day in prayer. A few minutes of silent prayer or reading from a prayer book in the morning, a few more in the evening, perhaps some Scripture reading during the day, and a moment of silent prayer before and after a meal doesn't sound like the life of an extremely religious person. But for a typical Amish adult there is always an awareness of God, not just in what they deny themselves for God but also in an appreciation of the blessings of everyday life.

Catching a glance of his wife's colorful flower garden as he passes his house during early morning chores, Amish minister Wayne Miller, of Millersburg, Ohio, comments in *A Day in the Life of the Amish,* "The dazzling array of flowers in the early morning does lift one's soul."[1] At the day's end, Yost Yoder gazes at the view of his St. Mary's, Ontario, farm and notes, "There's an almost full moon shin-

The Amish express their belief in and awareness of God through hard work, goodness in everyday life, and commitment to family.

ing in my window. Looking out, the scenery is simply gorgeous." He hears "the soft hoot of an owl from one of the maple trees in the lawn," as he wonders, "God has surely been good to us—do I appreciate all His goodness enough?"[2] An Amish woman putting careful stitches in her quilt contemplates Jesus as she works, a moment captured in the film *The Amish*. Their religion is woven into the fabric of their everyday lives.

Every other Sunday a different Amish home becomes a place of worship. When it comes to formal worship of God, the Old Order Amish still keep it simple. They consider church buildings another symbol of worldliness and pride, and their three-hour service is as plain as their Sunday church clothes: no candles, flowers, carved altars or pews, musical instruments, or any other fixtures we might associate with a church. Attendance is considered mandatory, barring illness or some other emergency.

You won't find any Old Order Amish preaching on a street corner or going door-to-door to teach others about their faith. They operate no soup kitchens or missions in depressed areas, though some families do host inner-city children on their farms during summer months. The Amish give generously to Red Cross blood drives, and different districts will reach out to needy non-Amish, as many did during the Midwest floods of 1993. In general, though, they are not looking for converts, and their faith is something they keep private. They are concerned about protecting their communities and following St. Paul's advice in the New Testament to be separate from the world. Unaccustomed to explaining their faith verbally, they simply live it, letting their actions be their religious statement.

The Amish still consider themselves Anabaptists who rejected the state churches of Europe hundreds of years ago for not being biblical enough. Their firm antimilitary stance stems from Jesus' call to "turn the other cheek." Early Christian church leaders Peter and Paul both admonished Christians to be apart from the world. Paul said that women's heads should always be covered, and they should be subservient to their husbands. The Amish dislike of being photographed is based partly on the Second Commandment warning against making "graven images," and partly on the notion that being photographed leads to pride, the most destructive of human vices described in the Bible. The Amish see themselves as similar to early Christians, who often joined the church as adults (sometimes entire families were baptized together) and who worshipped in each others' homes.

Each church district is autonomous, or self-governing. It has boundary lines that usually enclose a few square miles. In this space there are perhaps more than two dozen Amish families, which can mean more than two hundred people at a church service. A congregation bigger than that will likely be split in two so everyone can fit into one home for the church services. By keeping the district small, people are on a first-name basis with each other; the bishop and each district's ministers know all of their "flock" by name.

Church leaders—bishops, ministers, and deacons—are all men. Each district or congregation determines rules of the Ordnung it will follow, and the bishop enforces it, with the support of the congregation. The bishop also tries to resolve conflicts among church members, as well as performing weddings and baptisms. The congregation has two or three ministers, who give long sermons,

An Amish family may have more than two hundred people at their home for a church service.

without notes, during the church service, and who aid the bishop in leading the congregation.

The deacon reads Scripture and leads prayers at church services. He keeps track of alms funds for the congregation's needy and tries to remain aware of various families' needs. When a church member is known to be violating Old Order rules, the deacon pays the member a visit to investigate. He brings word of excommunication from the bishop to erring members who continue to flout rules, or word of reinstatement back into the church for those who are ready to give up whatever non-Amish behavior got them into trouble. The church leaders are seen as servants of their congregation and of God. None are paid or trained, and they are expected to perform their services in addition to whatever work they do to support their family.

The Amish method of selecting their church leaders is very different from other Christian religions. A man doesn't decide he has a "calling" to the ministry and then apply for a position. That notion sounds rather conceited to the Amish. In fact, attending a seminary for religious training is grounds for excommunication! Rather, when a new minister, bishop, or deacon is needed, he is chosen by lot.

In nominating someone for a church position, congregation members "look for humility and evidence of good farm and family management," according to Hostetler.[3] A minister must be a married man, and bishops are selected from among the ministers. If, say, six men are nominated for a minister's position, and all are considered worthy, a Bible verse on a slip of paper is put into one of six hymnals or prayer books. The man who selects the book with the verse gets the job, and it's considered God's will for that man to be chosen; it also helps the congregation avoid harmful disagreements in deciding who to appoint. Instead of congratulations from the congregation, the new minister receives their sympathy, for it is a job with much responsibility, and it is for life.

Amish homes, already large to accommodate a big family, traditionally have removable interior walls to provide an open area for the church service. Sometimes in newer homes a large basement is used. A family will host services once or twice a year. Knowing the entire congregation will be inside the house helps keep Amish church members from having something forbidden in their home. A set of wooden benches to provide seating during the service is transported by horse-drawn wagon around the church district, arriving at the designated house in time for a Sunday setup.

Before a family hosts a church service their house is likely to get a thorough cleaning, perhaps even a new paint job, and furniture is stored away to make room for the benches. They have a lot of cooking to do, with help from neighbors, because after the church service the entire congregation stays for lunch. Even the barn is spruced up and stocked with fresh hay for all the horses "visiting" that day.

People begin arriving at the "church house" shortly before the service begins at 9:00 A.M. Some people, of course, live close enough to walk. "Men and women enter the house by separate doors and sit apart," according to Kraybill, and they will eat lunch at separate tables.[4] Young children sit with parents of the same sex during the service.

The church service lasts three hours or more. It consists of hymns, two sermons, Scripture readings, prayers, and testimonials, or

Often a family can walk to a church service, because the homes in a community are close together.

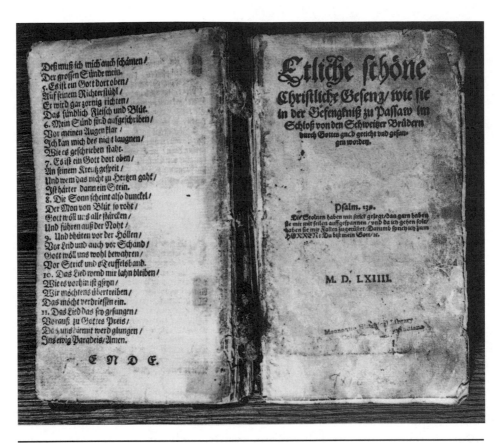

The *Ausbund is the oldest hymnal in continuous use in church history. This copy is from the year 1564.*

accounts from different church members reaffirming the day's preaching. The congregation sings hymns from the 460-year-old hymnal, the *Ausbund*, which has words only. The tunes are memorized and sung slowly. Sometimes one verse of a hymn can take twenty minutes to sing. While the congregation sings the second hymn the ministers decide who is to preach that morning, so the sermons are spontaneous and humbly introduced. The main sermon may last more than an hour, and when it's done the minister thanks the congregation for their attention and patience.

During the service, babies and children and even some tired adults doze off. Children use handkerchiefs to make "mice" or "twin babies in a cradle" shapes.[5] As the sermon goes on, cookies or crackers and water to drink are passed on a plate down the rows for the young children.

Men and women leave the service separately. While the men remove some benches and put other benches together to form tables, the women begin laying out a lunch of homemade or store-bought bread and butter, jam, cheese, pickles and pickled red beets, apple *schnitz* (a dessert), and coffee. It may take three or four table settings to feed everyone. Women and girls eat last, then wash up. It's a chance to visit with friends and neighbors. Leaving early, especially right after lunch, is considered rude.

There may be members from other church districts attending that day, or visiting ministers who take a turn preaching, but only if their districts are "in fellowship" with each other. To the casual observer, all Plain groups might look the same, but there are many subtle differences between church districts. (Plain groups include Old Order, Beachy, or New Order Amish, and other Anabaptist groups such as the Mennonites.) Groups in fellowship with each other interpret and practice plain living more or less the same and don't necessarily have to live within the same settlement. Old Order Amish groups in Ohio, Indiana, and Pennsylvania are in fellowship with one another in spite of a few differences, such as bicycle riding in the Midwest or the use of milking machines in Pennsylvania. By contrast, sometimes plain-dressing Amish living in the same area aren't in fellowship with one another.

In the tight-knit Amish communities, anyone who goes against the Ordnung is likely to be found out, whether it's for something like adultery, driving a car, wearing jewelry, or attending a Bible study with other Christians. As one Amish woman told Kraybill, "Everybody knows everything about everyone else."[6]

Most offenses will bring about a rebuke by the deacon or minister, and the offender will be expected to make a confession in church. For a minor issue, like wearing jewelry, they give their confession while sitting. They kneel if it's for something a bit more serious, such as, in some districts, riding in a hired car on a Sunday.

A more serious offense may result in a six-week ban followed by a kneeling confession during church, giving that member an idea of what it would be like to be shunned. Excommunication is immediate for offenses like adultery or buying a car, but only if it has the entire congregation's vote and only as a last resort. For example, someone caught using a computer often will be allowed to finish a big business project before having to give up it up. When offenders confess and apologize they are quickly forgiven, and those excommunicated can rejoin the church if they are willing to make a kneeling confession.

Shunning those who refuse to submit to church authority is awkward for all involved. The wife who continues to go to Bible studies after having been warned not to might be ignored at a family gathering, even by her husband, and will have to eat at a different table. As one Amish church member told Donald Kraybill, "If it weren't for shunning, many of our people would leave for a more progressive church where they could have electricity and cars."[7] Sometimes entire families do leave the church, either to go to a more or less conservative Amish affiliation, or possibly to attend a Mennonite church that allows the conveniences the Amish deny themselves.

Divisive church issues are dealt with head-on twice each year just prior to the spring and fall communion services. The services are not held until all members are in agreement on church matters. The church service before the scheduled communion service is six hours long (children are exempt), and members are expected to confess any violations of church rules or make amends with other members with whom they've had differences. If a church member is known to have violated a church rule and doesn't confess, he or she is denied communion. The communion services, which serve home-made bread and wine, are important milestones in the Amish calendar, for they signify unity among members.

THE ISSUE OF
EDUCATION

6

As much as the Amish have always tried to separate themselves from the world outside their community, Amish children, until recent years, had one thing in common with other children: their schools. A couple of generations ago, most rural American children attended small schools within walking distance of their homes. This fit in well with the Amish goal of small community settings. Also, since the Amish don't teach religion at school, sending their children to a public one didn't matter. Amish fathers, in fact, often served on the boards of the one- or two-room schools their children and the other local children attended.

But in the 1920s and 1930s, laws governing education in general became a greater priority in many states. Rural counties began consolidating their schools, or building one large, centrally located school to which most children needed to be bused. The Amish did not want to send their children, whom they wanted close to home, to this type of grade school with its big bureaucracy and less personal environment. What's more, they didn't want to send their children to high school, period. During several decades of conflict, the Amish struggled to implement the best solution to their dilemma. Most Amish communities today build, staff, and operate their own schools. With help offered from an outside group, the Amish, who usually don't allow themselves to use the court system, won permission from the Supreme Court in 1972 to educate their children with their own schools.

Today, a small white or brick schoolhouse on a quiet country road is as much a part of the Amish landscape as the horse and buggy. Amish parents can send their scholars off in the morning, lunch pail in hand, without facing a possible arrest, fine, or even jail sentence. Many of their grandparents weren't so lucky, as there were few Amish schools before 1960.

In 1921 Ohio legislators passed a compulsory education law requiring schooling through age eighteen. Five Amish fathers in northeast Ohio settlements were arrested in 1922 for neglecting their children's welfare by keeping them out of high school. Many of their children were made wards of the state and put in orphanages. That drastic situation lasted only two weeks, when the families involved agreed to follow the law. Some Ohio families were discouraged enough by the schooling situation—which followed problems with the draft during World War I—to leave the United States and attempt to form a settlement in Mexico (it didn't last). Most, though, complied with the new law, applying for work permits for their children at age sixteen.

By the 1930s, the trend toward school consolidation arrived in Lancaster County, Pennsylvania. The state legislature also made it mandatory to stay in school until age fifteen, that is, requiring a year

Schools are typically white or brick buildings with one or two rooms, as many American schools were in the 1800s and early 1900s.

of high school. A delegation of Amish men spent two years lobbying for religious freedom to have their children educated as they believed necessary. But by the end of 1937, many Amish fourteen-year-olds were literally hiding at home, and one father was jailed.

Working with state government, the Amish community in Lancaster County won the right to apply for work permits for fourteen-year-olds. But by 1949 the state raised the compulsory education age again, to sixteen. Several dozen Amish parents were jailed for not complying. A state legislator from Philadelphia urged Amish parents to "turn on your radio, the water, the light, the heat . . . the electric" and, in short, join the modern world.[1] By the mid-1950s the Lancaster County Amish reached a compromise with the state by operating their own vocational schools for Amish teens, and the matter was settled.

The education issue for the Amish received national attention in Iowa in 1965. Old Order Amish in Buchanan County established their own elementary schools with Amish teachers, rather than send children to the newer consolidated public school. Locally, it became a heated issue. On November 19, county school officials sent a bus to one of the Amish schools, planning to transport the students to a public elementary school. One of the Amish adults present shouted "Run!" in German to the children. Press photographers took pictures of children running for the nearby cornfields, and the photographs were published in papers nationwide. The state governor intervened, and many fines charged against the Amish parents were paid by anonymous donors as the issue quieted down.

A Lutheran minister in Michigan took interest in the Amish education struggle and, knowing they wouldn't defend themselves, formed the National Committee for Amish Religious Freedom

On November 19, 1965, Amish schoolchildren in Hazelton, Iowa, ran and hid in a cornfield rather than allow themselves to be bused to a public elementary school.

School serves to reinforce community ties, as the students remain with each other and with the same teacher for years.

(NCARF). Its members included Jewish and Christian leaders as well as lawyers and educators. Though the situation in Iowa had been resolved, NCARF got a chance to take the Amish education issue to court in Kansas, a case which they lost and which the Supreme Court refused to review. Their next chance came in Green County, Wisconsin, where three Old Order fathers (one an Amish Mennonite) were jailed for keeping their children out of high school. Losing on the local level, this case did reach the Supreme Court by 1971. In 1972 the high court ruled in favor of the Amish operating schools according to their own customs. As Chief Justice Warren E. Burger noted, the Amish were not an economic "burden" to American society, in spite of their eighth-grade education.

What exactly were the Amish protesting, as American rural education began changing? The Old Order Amish wanted to preserve a lot: a local school, with no busing; a small school, with local control that would include Amish parents' participation; an eight-month school year (which still has the required number of school days), so children could help their families during planting and harvest season; and teachers who understood Amish life and values. There were also many things they didn't want: sex education and teaching about evolution; too much "book learning," as opposed to hands-on teaching of practical skills; and too much exposure to non-Amish peers and values.

Today, the Amish school is an extension of the Amish child's home and community life. Schools generally have one or two rooms, with no electricity but many windows for light. Each child has the same teacher, typically an unmarried Amish woman, who truly gets to know the students she sees year after year. Unlike teachers in other schools, an Amish schoolteacher has no more than an eighth-grade formal education herself, if she's Amish.

In her book about an Amish school, former teacher Sara E. Fisher reprinted parts of an eighth-grade student's diary, which talked about the girl's last year of school. It was the girl's first year in an Amish school recently built by church members. She went to the new school with thirty-nine other scholars, and she wrote, "It certainly seems different from a public school because you know all the people." Another difference for her was the interaction between grades and age levels, something an Amish school encourages. Older students help younger ones, who are new to the English being spoken in school and who "learn a lot by listening to the upper grades." Students also are involved in the upkeep of the school, and at the day's end "the boys take turns carrying coal and taking ashes [from the stove] out, and also help us sweep or mop the schoolhouse." Early in the fall, older students may be excused from school after half a day to help with farmwork at home. The teacher arrives early in the day to start up the coal furnace, and as students arrive they place their lunches on top of it. By noon the school is packed with the aroma of baked potatoes or homemade pizza.

The girl wrote in her diary that she was eagerly anticipating the upcoming Christmas program, something Amish schools have added to their school calendar in recent years. Names were drawn for a gift exchange, and with their parents attending, children performed songs, skits the scholars wrote themselves, and poems. There is no mention of Santa Claus or Christmas trees and no applause for the performances (all seen as distractions or signs of showiness).

Winter recess meant indoor board games like Monopoly or Sorry. "Some of the boys brought their sleds along . . . and some-

times, of course, we have snow battles!" Cards and special lunches
were exchanged on St. Valentine's Day in February, and in March, on
an "afternoon when it wasn't quite so cold we went for a walk up
the road to go and sing for an old lady, which was fun." During the

school year, the students get little or no homework, because they have plenty of chores at home.

In April, the scholars visited another local Amish school, where "they sang for us, and we watched them have a few classes, and then we had a friendly game of baseball." Another nice spring day included "a sort of informal nature lesson" with a hike in the woods. Eighth-grade graduation was a part of the end-of-the-year school picnic in May. All the scholars' families attended, and scholars challenged fathers to a baseball game. The girl planned to attend vocational school for a half day each week until her fourteenth birthday, to satisfy Pennsylvania education requirements, and then her schooling would be complete.[2]

Sociologist John Hostetler cited studies in his book *Amish Society* showing that Amish children score slightly better than the national average on standardized tests, in spite of having no television at home, small libraries, and teachers with no college training. Amish children tend to see their parents as role models, and Hostetler writes, "Amish children in the eighth grade rate their families more positively than do non-Amish children." He quoted test results showing Amish children to be, in general, "quiet, friendly, responsible, and conscientious." Another test "reveals a strong awareness of other people."[3]

Teachers are selected by apparent aptitude and serve as apprentices before having their own classroom. Teachers from several districts meet occasionally during the year. Like the Amish students themselves, younger teachers learn from the more experienced ones. An Amish publishing company in Ontario puts out a magazine for Amish teachers that exchanges ideas and techniques. Schools are financed by taxes that Amish parents and property owners pay among themselves, and school buildings are built by volunteers in the church district.

Children learn English and basic arithmetic, as well as some history, geography, and health. There is also much singing throughout the week. Science classes may be limited to nature studies or practical sciences that can be applied in everyday Amish life. The schools do not teach religion. That is considered the job of parents. Nevertheless, some Bible verses may be read and prayers recited at school. Memorizing facts is preferred over discussing different ideas, and competition between scholars is discouraged. The Old Order Amish have developed their own texts in which readers will find no sex education, fairy tales, or stories with talking animals or mention of magic.

Children are not praised for their natural talents or punished for their academic weaknesses. Teachers try to use rewards more than punishments. For the Amish youth who enjoys school, finishing at age fourteen may be difficult, but to "become a committed Amish person, a boy or girl who likes school for its own sake must learn to be indifferent to it," writes Hostetler.[4] Those who decide to pursue more education and become what Hostetler calls Amish "dropouts" usually don't attend high school, because it is so different from what they are used to. Rather, they tend to wait a few years and finish their education as young adults. Donald Kraybill wrote of a former Amish woman who described her tearful meeting in a cornfield with her bishop. The bishop was compelled to excommunicate her for attending college to become a social worker. But students who enjoy school and do remain Amish find many outlets for their academic learning. Their people continue to look for ways to support themselves and interact with the world on a limited basis while they maintain their communities.

WHAT DO THE AMISH READ?

Several publications are produced by and for the Amish. They provide news about different communities, advice on day-to-day life, and confirmation for many Amish of the value of their way of life.

In *Family Life*, a housewife writes tips on saving money. Don't buy paper towels, use a dishcloth at the table. Similarly, don't buy chocolate chips or raisins, but just make plain cookies. She ends, however, with these words: "Though I am concerned about not spending my husband's money unwisely, I also believe there are more important things in life than pinching every penny that comes my way."

In a monthly publication called *The Diary: of the Old Order Churches*, a teenager writes in about a group of friends making "comforts" for Romanians. Also, young teens were looking for Amish pen pals.

The teachers' magazine, *Blackboard Bulletin*, runs a regular feature called "Brushing up on Pronunciation." It tells Amish teachers how to pronounce certain English words they seldom use, such as "fatigue" or "rapport."

Amish adults have two newspapers, the *Budget* and the more conservative *Die Botschaft* ("The Message"). The Budget has a circulation of more than twenty thousand and is made up almost entirely of reports about goings-on in different Amish church districts across the United States and Canada. Each district has a volunteer "scribe" who sends news in to the newspaper. Reports describe the current weather in that area, then mention visitors to the district, weddings or births, or unusual events.

The goal of an Amish farm family is to support itself, not to make a lot of money. A small farm cultivated with horse-drawn equipment can still serve this end.

TRADITION IN THE MODERN WORLD

7

A long with horses and plain clothing, another important symbol of Amish life has been the farm: clean white farmhouses with a colorful garden, a neat yard, and adjoining fields cultivated in tidy rows. But while horses and plain clothing have remained constant symbols, farming as a vocation among the Amish isn't as automatic as it used to be. The Amish population continues to grow as available farmland dwindles, especially in increasingly developed areas like Lancaster County, Pennsylvania. The Amish have become creative, looking for ways to support their families, keep both parents close by, and still live a rural life.

Amish farms have always been small compared to modern farms: 60 to 80 acres (24 to 32 ha) was plenty for one family to handle with horse-drawn farm equipment. An Amish family's aim is to support itself, rather than become wealthy, so large-scale farming or excessive growth in any kind of business is discouraged. One way the Amish have supplied more farms is by splitting them: an 80-acre (32 ha) farm becomes two 40-acre (16 ha) farms. As a result, the land is used more intensely, and the population becomes denser.

The early Anabaptists were not originally farmers. As outcasts in Europe, they often were allowed to stay in certain areas only if they were willing to farm and revitalize vacant land. Before long it was an arrangement they began to appreciate. The Anabaptists found many Bible passages about stewardship, or wise use and care of the earth. It is described as a gift from and duty to God, so they set out to do it well.

In time the Amish Anabaptists became known as the best farmers in Europe. They improved soil by rotating crops, used natural fertilizers, and grew clover and alfalfa. Their reputation as good farmers continued in America. The Amish considered farming ideal, and still do, because they see the earth as a gift from God, they value hard work, and both parents are able to be at home. Though the original Anabaptists were educated townspeople, one of the reasons today's Amish shun higher education is their fear that it would teach their young people to hate hard work. In the Amish community, it is the successful farmer who will enjoy high prestige.

While the Amish have struggled to determine how to use technology in their homes, how to use it on the farm has presented other problems. Amish farmers must compete with non-Amish farmers in selling their farm products. To keep up, some allowances for technology have been made in many Amish districts.

Some eastern Amish farmers tried tractors in their fields in the early 1920s. Then the tractors were completely banned in 1923. Not only would the tractor replace men and horses, it was reasoned, but it might lead to wanting cars as well. This doesn't mean you won't find a tractor on an Amish farm. The Amish *do* use them for a job like pulling out tree stumps, or the engines are used to power

The debate over using technology has led to some unusual compromises. In some eastern communities, for example, farmers use harvesting equipment, but only if it is pulled by horses or mules.

pumps, feed grinders, or ventilation fans. In the fields, they often use modern farm machines like hay balers, as long as the machinery is pulled by a horse. They use other machines, too, as long as the machines use a power source other than the local electric company. Power can come from hydraulic air pressure, bottled gas, or batteries. The Amish will use modern technology, but it isn't to be used just to cut back on physical work.

Men, women, children, and horses do most of the work on an Amish farm. A non-Amish farmer who uses a combine for harvesting makes it a one-person job. In the process, more than $100,000 could be invested in that machine alone. On the other hand, an Amish farmer uses simpler machinery and has to invest only $800 to $2,800 for a good horse and horse-drawn machinery. Cost isn't the only advantage. Amish farmers like to point out that, unlike tractors, the horse gives back something useful to the farmer: manure. And a horse reproduces itself.

For the Amish, farming isn't just about making a living while utilizing God's gift of nature. It's also about depending on one another. Though husbands and wives have separate roles on the farm, they are both needed to make it work. The wife often handles family finances, in addition to all her other responsibilities. Farming without tractors also leaves jobs available for younger men who are saving money for their future. Church districts have split over tractor usage. Not allowing them is more than just a matter of rejecting a certain kind of technology. It also means a rejection of the bigger debt Amish farmers would go into if they used them.

Even though farming is considered the ideal vocation among the Amish, not all families can do it. These days, more and more men work as painters or carpenters, for example. Some also supply their

Some Amish have left farming to take on other vocations. This man has become an accomplished clock maker.

communities with items that used to be commonplace but that nobody makes anymore. Blacksmiths shoe horses, and others make buggies or buggy wheels. Some Amish mechanics make a living by rigging appliances like washing machines to be adapted for the power sources used by the Amish. Some families run a small business in addition to farming, if necessary.

In land-scarce Lancaster County, Sam Stoltzfus quit farming and sold his cows to his oldest son. Sam and his wife gave up the house to their son, too. They built a daadi house on the property and now sell gazebos and horseradish. Sam doesn't mind the change, though. "I was never such a good farmer," he says. In Holmes County, Ohio, Lester Beachy grabbed the chance to buy a noodle business when it became available. After working for many years in a cabinet shop, he now runs the noodle business at home with the help of three employees.

In Arthur, Illinois, Andy and Vera Jess and their six children have several jobs. Andy works for a door manufacturer, one daughter works in a door shop, and a son works in a factory. Vera cooks and serves meal to tourists who visit their settlement, and the whole family makes painted wooden toy animals to sell. In more lenient Amish districts, telephones for business use have become widespread, sometimes within easy reach on a desktop. As Sam Stoltzfus put it, "the one with the phone gets the business."

Young Amish men or women who are working and saving for their future, or helping their families financially, prefer to have an Amish employer. A non-Amish factory or restaurant wouldn't be as flexible about letting employees off for an Amish wedding (usually held on Tuesdays or Thursdays) or a funeral. And church leaders discourage youth from taking jobs that would give them too much exposure to non-Amish peers.

Many Amish women sell garden produce at roadside stands.

It is more common today for Amish wives to earn incomes, usually in businesses that are compatible to their domestic roles. Many sell garden produce or homemade crafts, things they can produce while they stay at home with their children. One Pennsylvania Amish woman worked at a bakery before she married. When her

The Amish have attracted many tourists who are more interested in getting an unusual photograph of them than learning why they live as they do.

nine children were between the ages of two and seventeen, she figured her own bakery would both earn money and teach her children about a business while keeping them busy. The Amish are expected to keep their businesses relatively small. Some are wealthy, but most consider extra business growth a sign of pride, not a necessity.

Since the 1940s, tourism has increased a great deal and helped the Amish financially. This has been a mixed blessing. On the one hand, tourism provides a large outlet for Amish products, which helps since fewer Amish farm for a living. On the other hand, these naturally reserved and quiet plain folk find themselves the object of sometimes rude fascination, as tourists drive up and down their country roads by the busload. Perhaps the biggest objection the Amish have to tourists is their "shutter fingers," or determination to take souvenir photographs. These photographers are either ignorant of or insensitive to the Amish dislike of being photographed. A farmer in Indiana said it can make one feel like a "zoo animal." Lancaster County, an easy drive from the large urban centers of Philadelphia, Baltimore, and New York City, draws the biggest tourist crowd: five million visitors spending a total of $400 million each year!

In the late 1940s and early 1950s, car travel became very popular. Americans were emerging from two great crises, the Great Depression in the 1930s and World War II in the 1940s. They sought new forms of recreation, such as getting out to see the country. In the 1950s the Amish received wide attention over the schooling issue, and outsiders began getting curious. Today, Amish people in heavily visited areas are used to being an attraction. Sometimes, though, they will cancel trips into town during the summer tourist season, and some post No Tourist signs on schools or repair shops. The Amish don't intend to be unfriendly; in fact, they often enjoy chance visits with outsiders. But as one man told Hostetler, "If we waved at every tourist, we would soon have a sore arm."[1]

As the Amish rely less on farming, they are influenced more by the world. Some must think about daily production instead of yearly seasons. Whatever an Amish man or woman does to make a living, one thing they must always keep in mind is: how will this affect my family and, ultimately, my community? To work hard and earn a living is important to every Amish person. But to maintain their family and community life must be the goal.

COMMITMENTS
TO THE FUTURE

8

While spring and summer are perhaps the busiest times of the year for most Amish families because of their rural lifestyles, it is during the fall months that the most important events in the community take place. Baptism of new, committed church members often takes place in September. Later in the fall, especially November, come weddings, with their promise of another family to carry on Amish tradition.

Baptism is very significant because it means a young adult, age eighteen or older, is rejecting a life in the world—perhaps having tasted a few of its conveniences and entertainments—and *choosing* to commit themselves to the Amish life. It takes place during a Sunday service. Writing about a baptism ceremony, held in a barn on a bright September morning, Hostetler described the six young women about to become church members: "Each sits with bowed head, as though in deep meditation and prayer for the lifelong vow about to be taken. None dares to risk a glimpse at the audience or to gaze about, for it is a solemn occasion. Their clothing is strictly uniform: black organdy caps, black dresses, white organdy capes, long white organdy aprons, black stockings, and black oxfords."

Two hours later, after two sermons, the young women kneel before the bishop. He asks each a few questions, to which they answer "yes." After a prayer, the deacon's wife removes the first woman's cap. The bishop lays his hands on her head, declaring, in German, "Upon your faith, which you have confessed before God and these many witnesses, you are baptized in the name of the Father, the Son, and the Holy Spirit. Amen." The bishop cups his hands over the woman's head, and the deacon pours a cupful of water through them, which trickles down over the woman's hair and face. The bishop's wife "greets the new member with the Holy Kiss." When all are baptized, "a few tears are brushed aside as they retie their covering (cap) strings." Altogether, the service lasts about four hours.[1]

In Lester Beachy's church district in Holmes County, Ohio, those undergoing baptism are asked, "Do you promise, in the presence of God and his church, with the Lord's help, to support these doctrines and regulations, to earnestly fill your place in the church, to help counsel and labor, and not to depart from the same, come what may, life or death?"[2] The answer to that question must, of course, be yes.

A month or two later, in October or November, Amish church members can expect to hear, during another Sunday service, an announcement of a marriage coming up in the next two weeks. A wedding will be much anticipated, not just because it is an enjoyable

94

event for church members to attend, but because it means a new family will help continue the Amish way of life.

The traditions surrounding an Amish engagement and wedding have little in common with the weddings that are announced in daily newspapers, with photographs of brides in beautiful gowns. In some districts an Amish engagement is official when, as a formality, the deacon or minister goes to the future bride's home to get her parents' "consent" to the marriage, though actually it's already been decided. When the wedding is announced at church a week or two before the ceremony, the groom-to-be leaves just before the congregation sings the last hymn. He is headed for his fiancée's home, where he will help with preparations until the wedding.

Here's how an Amish woman from northwest Ohio described, in *A Day in the Life of the Amish,* some preparations for her daughter's wedding in a few days:

> Before sunrise, I was in the garden digging the last of the potatoes and watching the sun come up. It was such a lovely sight and good time to meditate.
>
> William [her husband] will not to go work this week, as there is far too much work to be done around home with only one thing on our minds: the wedding!
>
> He came to the garden and advised me to let Albert (Mary Louise's fiancé) dig the rest of the potatoes. . . . I went to help Samuel, our youngest son, sweep the new 40- x 64-foot machine shed where the ceremony will be held. It was built this summer, and the cement is still easy to clean. Samuel soon left for work. . . . I was not alone long

when Albert and the girls [the family's other daughters] were at my heels reporting a fair crop of potatoes, which will help feed the 500 guests that we are expecting to attend the wedding.

William came home with the bench wagon—a boxed-in vehicle which contains enough benches, song books and dishes to be used when church services are held in the home. Then we all joined together in the shed, sweeping, mopping and arranging things to allow lots of needed room.

That week there would be "26 cooks to help prepare the homecooked meal of mashed potatoes, chicken gravy, dressing, ham, mixed vegetables, noodles, coleslaw, cheese, . . . and lime Jell-O," as well as three kinds of pies and more than two dozen cakes. One neighbor who offered to help was sent flour, fifteen dozen eggs collected "from our flock of 20 hens," and other supplies to make the noodles.[3]

An Amish wedding will make no use of caterers, florists, musicians, bartenders, jewelers, reception halls, or church buildings. Like the Sunday church services, it will be plain and home based. While the bride's family provides the large wedding dinner at their home, the groom has had his share of work to do, too. In addition to helping with wedding preparations, he is in charge of inviting his family members, in person or by mail. It is considered an honor to be invited to help cook and serve the meal (parents of the bride and groom will not actually work on the wedding day) and both men and women will share those jobs. Amish weddings and their traditions will vary from area to area, but following are the preparations

Weddings, like church services, take place in the home.

and ceremony for a wedding in central Pennsylvania Hostetler attended.

Thirty cooks, all married couples, arrived at the bride's home at 7:00 A.M. the day before the wedding to get to work. "Custom required that the bridegroom cut off the heads of the fowl," and after the men plucked the chickens, ducks, and turkeys, the women prepared them for cooking. There were potatoes to peel, hot water to haul in, nuts to crack, garbage to take out, and temporary pine-board tables to build.

The wedding itself was to take place at a neighbor's home a mile away. On the wedding day the bride, groom, and two other attending couples arrived before dawn. The bridal couple's clothing was in the same style as church clothes but new. The home was filled with guests when the ceremony began at 9:00 A.M.

As guests sang wedding hymns from the *Ausbund*, the couple was instructed by the bishop on the duties of marriage. Then, with all seated, the bishop preached at length about marriages from the Bible, beginning with Adam and Eve. Around noon he asked the young couple, who were holding hands, to step forward. Within a few minutes they made their vows and the "bishop pronounced them husband and wife. Many, including the bishop, wiped away their tears, for all understood that the marriage would remain until death."[4]

When bride, groom, and their attending couples reached the bride's home, there were no shouts of joy or congratulations, and no one threw rice or confetti; the atmosphere was serious. During the dinner, the bridal party sat at a corner table decorated with pretty dishes and half a dozen decorated cakes. Their goblets were filled with cider from an antique wine flask. The other guests used regular dishes. A silent prayer was said before the first group of guests ate. When they were finished eating, their dishes were quickly washed in laundry tubs and set back on the tables for the next sitting.

Rather than take a honeymoon, the young married couple may spend a few weeks visiting relatives. Though the wedding day is much quieter than that of a non-Amish wedding, it is a happy day. Youth of courting age especially enjoy it, as it reinforces goals they may have for their own futures as Amish church and community members.

What does the future hold for those young Amish? While the Amish people grow in number and hold fast to their traditions, they also undergo subtle changes. Today's Amish must turn to different methods of supporting their families from what their parents or grandparents did. Lester Beachy expressed his concern that "there are so many different jobs that the Amish are employed in compared to years gone by. This is a threat to our lifestyle. Many in this area are considering the possibility of relocating to different areas in search of more land and cheaper land," in order to "keep the men at home on the farm to preserve our family structure."[5]

When changes seem to come too easily, some families do indeed up and move. They may have particularly strong feelings about some issues, such as rowdy courting practices among Amish youth. Families will move to more conservative settlements, or even join with other like-minded families to begin new ones.

New trends can occur when someone tries something new, such as a machine hooked up to hydraulic power or even a computer plugged into an alternative energy source. When it's discovered by the bishop but ignored (what is ignored and what isn't will vary from district to district), then others begin using the innovation, too. The Amish home today that has a gas-powered refrigerator or indoor bathroom, or the barn that may have a bulk milk tank or even a telephone, are quite different from homes and barns of fifty years ago. Such changes come as the Amish experiment with technology and the Ordnung.

While some Amish groups bemoan what may seem to be too many changes, it is their flexibility in dealing with the changing world around them that has helped the Amish communities survive. The persistent question is whether those communities will survive an increasing amount of outside influence.

Sam Stoltzfus, of Lancaster County, realizes a lot has changed in his own church district, but he is optimistic. In a publication called *Pennsylvania Folklife,* Stoltzfus wrote about his church district of eighty-four people in which less than half of the twenty-three "church places" are now farms:

> A "For Sale" sign goes up along South Ronks Road. In due time the property is sold and the family moves to Perry County, Pennsylvania, because of the potential for more growth there. But a young married couple moves into the house, so there is still potential for growth here, too. So, no doubt as long as the Pequea Creek keeps flowing through the Pequea Valley, the Amish church in the area will keep growing.[6]

SOURCE NOTES

Chapter Three

1. Kraybill, Donald B., *The Riddle of the Amish Culture* (Baltimore: Johns Hopkins University Press, 1989), p. 95.
2. Ibid., p. 29.
3. *A Day in the Life of the Amish* (Greendale, Wis.: Reiman Publications, 1994), p. 25.
4. Kraybill, p. 100.

Chapter Four

1. Kraybill, Donald B., *The Riddle of the Amish Culture* (Baltimore: Johns Hopkins University Press, 1989), p. 73.
2. Bender, Sue, *Plain and Simple: A Woman's Journey to the Amish* (New York: HarperCollins, 1989), p. 76.
3. Ibid., p. 122.
4. Kraybill, p. 185.

5. *A Day in the Life of the Amish* (Greendale, Wis.: Reiman Publications, 1994), p. 59.

6. Fisher, Sara E., and Rachel K. Stahl, *The Amish School* (Intercourse, Penn.: Good Books, People's Place, 1989), p. 37.

Chapter Five

1. *A Day in the Life of the Amish* (Greendale, Wis.: Reiman Publications, 1994), p. 29.

2. Ibid., p. 35.

3. Hostetler, John, *Amish Society,* 4th edition (Baltimore: Johns Hopkins University Press, 1993), pp. 105–106.

4. Kraybill, Donald B., *The Riddle of the Amish Culture* (Baltimore: Johns Hopkins University Press, 1989), p. 103.

5. Hostetler, p. 216.

6. Kraybill, p. 92.

7. Ibid., p. 117.

Chapter Six

1. Kraybill, Donald B., *The Riddle of the Amish Culture* (Baltimore: Johns Hopkins University Press, 1989), p. 125.

2. Fisher, Sara E., and Rachel K. Stahl, *The Amish School* (Intercourse, Penn.: Good Books, People's Place, 1989), pp. 47–53.

3. Hostetler, John, *Amish Society,* 4th edition (Baltimore: Johns Hopkins University Press, 1993), p. 188.

4. Ibid., p. 312.

Chapter Seven

1. Hostetler, John, *Amish Society,* 4th edition (Baltimore: Johns Hopkins University Press, 1993), p. 318.

Chapter Eight

1. Hostetler, John, *Amish Society,* 4th edition (Baltimore: Johns Hopkins University Press, 1993), pp. 79–81.
2. Letter to author.
3. *A Day in the Life of the Amish* (Greendale, Wis.: Reiman Publications, 1994), p. 43.
4. Hostetler, pp. 194–196.
5. Letter to author.
6. *Pennsylvania Folklife: The Amish* 43:3 (Spring 1994), p. 131.

FOR FURTHER READING

Denlinger, A. Martha. *Real People: Amish and Mennonites in Lancaster County, Pennsylvania*. Scottdale, Penn.: Herald Press, 1986.

Good, Merle and Phyllis. *Twenty Most Asked Questions About the Amish*. Intercourse, Penn.: Good Books, 1979.

Foster, Sally. *Where Time Stands Still*. Northbrook, Ill.: Dodd, Mead & Co., 1987.

Hostetler, John A., ed. *Amish Roots: A Treasury of History, Wisdom, and Lore*. Baltimore: Johns Hopkins University Press, 1989.

Kenna, Kathleen. *A People Apart*. Illustrated by Andrew Stawicki. Boston: Houghton Mifflin, 1996.

Kraybill, Donald. *Old Order Amish: Their Enduring Way of Life*. Photographs by Lucian Niemeyer. Baltimore: Johns Hopkins University Press, 1993.

Meyer, Carolyn. *Amish People: Plain Living in a Complex World*. New York: Atheneum, 1976.

Nolt, Steven M. *A History of the Amish*. Intercourse, Penn.: Good Books, 1992.

Pellman, Rachel and Kenneth. *The World of Amish Quilts.* Intercourse, Penn.: Good Books, 1984.

Saunders, Doreen Lynn. *Amish Quilts Designs.* New York: Dover Publications, 1990.

Swander, Mary. *Out of this World: A Woman's Life Amongst the Amish.* New York: Viking, 1995.

Yoder, Doyle. *America's Amish Country.* Berlin, Ohio: America's Amish Country Publications, 1992.

INTERNET SITES

Due to the changeable nature of the Internet, sites appear and disappear very quickly. Following are examples of the myriad of resources that provide useful information on the Amish and Mennonite churches. Internet addresses must be entered exactly as they appear.

The Pennsylvania Dutch Country Welcome Center has a Web page that features an "Ask the Amish" option. This site provides a good survey of Amish culture:

http://padutch.welcome.com/amish.html

The General Conference Mennonite Church Web page describes the fellowship of more than four hundred Mennonite congregations throughout North and South America. Sources explore the history, goals, activities, and news of the church:

http://www2.southwind.net/~gcmc

The Mennonite Central Committee, with seven hundred volunteers in fifty developing countries, is the relief and development arm of the North American Mennonite and Brethren in Christ churches. Their Web site describes their activities in food relief, agriculture, education, and social services:

http://www.mennonitecc.ca/mcc

INDEX

ABOUT THE AUTHOR

Jean Kinney Williams grew up in Ohio and lives there now with her husband and four children. She studied journalism in college and, in addition to writing, enjoys reading, volunteering at church, and spending time with her family. She is the author of the Franklin Watts First Book *Matthew Hensen: Polar Adventurer* (1994) and of another American Religious Experience book, *The Mormons* (1996).